HOPS: THEIR HISTORY, BOTANY, CHEMISTRY AND MEDICINAL USES

BY

P. L. SIMMONDS

British Library Cataloguing-in-Publication Data
A catalogue record for this book is available from the
British Library

CONTENTS

Peter Lund Simmonds

Peter Lund Simmonds was born in 1814, in Denmark, but lived in England for almost all his life. Simmonds founded the influential publication *Simmonds' Colonial Magazine and Foreign Miscellany,* which was incredibly popular with the Victorian public. It contained articles on the British Empire's colonies, as well as contemporary economic issues; especially with regards to the booming British East India Company. In addition to this editorial career, Simmonds penned many of his own scientific considerations about food, agriculture, international trade and polar exploration. One of the most notable texts was *The Curiosities of Food, Or, The Dainties and Delicacies of Different Nations Obtained from the Animal Kingdom.* This manuscript, published in 1859, caused substantial contemporary debate, portraying the human race as an all-hungry pestilence on the rest of the globe. Essentially, it was an encyclopaedia of consumption during the Victorian period, and detailed their eating habits - from the usual; birds animals and fish, to the bizarre; worms, bats, parchment paper, even leather clothing and dirt. This interest in conspicuous consumption led Simmonds to write a further scientific study; *The Savings of Science,* published in *Popular Science Monthly* in October 1883, in which he made a plea for recycling of waste. Simmonds supplicated for greater attention to the by-products of scientific research, arguing that 'the beautiful aniline dye, produced from the tar of the gas-works, is not more an example of the utilization of waste than beet-root sugar, obtained from what, a century ago, was a weed growing by the sea-side.' He also wrote on more everyday subjects, such as *Eggs in Chemistry and Commerce,* which came out six years later, in 1889. Simmonds died in 1897, at the age of eighty-three.

HISTORY, BOTANY, ECONOMIC USES, AND CHEMISTRY OF HOPS

THE hop, so extensively cultivated here and in other countries for the use of the brewer, and so well known to every housekeeper for culinary use, was not unknown to the ancients, being mentioned by the Arabian physician Mesué, who lived about 845, Hops were apparently first used for beer in Germany and in the Dutch breweries about the year 1400, their properties and uses being well understood. It was introduced into England from Flanders in 1524, but its strobiles were not used to preserve English beer, until about the year 1600. Henry VIII., in 1530, forbade the breweries to mix hops in their beer, and somewhat later Parliament was petitioned by Londoners to prohibit their use, "as they would spoil the taste of the drink, and endanger the people."

Beckmann ('Hist. of Inv.,' vol. iv. p. 386) states that plantations of hops had begun to be formed in England A.D. 1552. They are first mentioned in the English Statute-book in that year, viz, in the 5th and 6th Edward VI., c, 5 (repealed 5 Eliz., c. 2), an Act directing that land formerly in tillage should again be so cultivated, but excepting, amongst other ground, "land set with saffron or hops;" and by an Act of Parliament of the first year of James I., anno 1603, c. 18, it appears that hops were then produced in abundance in England.

In the oldest book I know about hops (Reynolde Scot's 'Perfite Platforme of a Hoppe Garden'), dated 1574, and printed in black letter, with many prefaces terminating in inverted pyramids of type, Kent is spoken of as the county of hops. The system of cultivation appears to have little changed since then; and the book, if it were not written in the style of an Act of Parliament, and interlarded with moral reflections and allusions to every poet and orator of ancient times, might have been written in the present day. Yet hops, at that date, were but of recent cultivation. For ages, while our ancestors were wont to flavour their ale with ground ivy, and honey, and various bitters, a weed called "hop" had been known about the hedges of England; but no one thought to cultivate it for brewing until the beginning of the sixteenth century. Some say the cultivated plant came first from Flanders, where it was certainly used before our brewers knew its virtues. In France, hop gardens are very ancient. Mention is made of them in some of the oldest records, though what the hops were used for does not appear. In England it had many enemies to contend with at first.

The leafy cone-like catkins or imbricated heads (strobili) of the common hop (*Humulus lupulus*, Lin.), a diœcious plant, with a perennial root, have long been an important article of commerce, and the culture and trade are becoming more and more extensive. The scales are scattered over with resinous spherical glands, which are easily rubbed off, and have a powerful agreeable odour and bitter taste; they appear to consist of an acid, ethereal oil, an aromatic resin, wax, extractive, and a bitter principle called lupuline. By pressure, hop heads yield a green, light, acrid oil, called oil of hops.

The aggregate fruits of this plant are botanically known under the name of strobiles, in common parlance as hops. These fruits consist of scales (bracts) and achaenia, the latter of which are surrounded by yellowish aromatic glands. They are usually termed lupulinic glands, and are the most active part of hops. They contain a volatile oil, and a bitter principle called *lupuline*, or *lupulite*, to the presence of which hops owe their properties. The bracts also contain some lupuline, and are therefore not devoid altogether of active principles.

The female flowers, growing on a separate plant, are in the form of a catkin, having each pair of flowers supported by a bract, which is ovate, acute, tubular at base. Sepal solitary, obtuse, smaller than the bract, and enfolding the ovary. Ovary roundish, compressed; stigmas two, long, subulate, downy. The bracts enlarge into a persistent catkin, each bract enclosing a nut enveloped in its permanent bractlet, and several grains of yellow lupuline.

To the folioles or scales of the flower of the hop adhere a

certain quantity of yellow powder or dust. Ives attributes to this powder alone the active principle of hops. But Payen and Chevallier are of opinion that the entire flower contains the same active principles which are found in the yellow dust. If this were not so, the hops, which in transport lose a great quantity of this yellow powder, would have but a feeble effect in the manufacture of beer.

As the quality of hops depends largely upon the amount of lupuline they contain, care is necessary to select those which have been fully matured on the vine before picking, when the lupuline will be found in much greater abundance, and of better quality. When derived from the fresh hop, it is of a very brilliant light lemon colour, almost transparent, and of a very strong aromatic odour. When rubbed between the fingers the grains are very easily broken, and adhere to the fingers, but on exposure to the light, or when from older hops, it becomes darker in colour, more opaque, and less gummy when rubbed between the fingers, according to the age. Owing to the difficulty of separating the powder from new hops (from the tendency it has to adhere to the scales, because of the resinous exudation with which it is coated, making its yield by mechanical process smaller), and the comparatively high price of new hops, as compared with old, making it less remunerative, the powder is mostly obtained from old hops. When the hop becomes old, the resinous exudation coating the lupuline concretes, and no longer adheres to the leaf, so that it can be easily separated by whipping the strobiles and sifting. When hops have become a year old, or as soon as the new crop comes into market, they are called old, and command only about one-half the price of the new crop. When two years old, they are called old-olds, and are still less valuable; and when five years old are considered worthless to brewers, although they still contain the lupuline, which possesses a part of its bitterness, but is destitute of volatile oil.

The age of hops can be told pretty accurately until they have attained three years; after that it is very doubtful.

Daring the first year they retain their bright green colonr and fine, strong aromatic smell, and the lupuline is bright yellow.

The second year they become darker, more dead-like, losing their bright colour, and have a sweet, slightly cheesy odour, which is due to the oxidation of the volatile oil, converting it into valerianic acid. The lupuline is of a golden yellow colour.

The third year the colour is not much changed, but the odour becomes faint, with the same cheesy smell. The lupuline is of a dark yellow or reddish tint.

The female plant, which is the object of careful cultivation, on account of its bitter and odorous strobiles employed in brewing, is much richer in principles than the male plant, from which it is distinguished by its aromatic, tonic, and narcotic properties; qualities which are combined in no other substance.

Economic Uses of Hops.—The roots and the stem of this plant merit also attention, as they furnish a raw material, presenting the planter with a secondary useful product.

The roots removed with the plant in the course of plucking, and which are generally thrown away, not only contain a starchy substance, which may be converted into glucose and alcohol, but also a large proportion of tannin, which the tanneries might use with advantage. This substance also offers a good material for making excellent paper-pulp and cardboard.

The stem possesses useful qualities; vegetable wax can be obtained from it, also a sap from which a durable reddish-brown can be made, and its ash is used in the manufacture of the Bohemian glass. Like the roots, it furnishes a very solid pulp for paper and cardboard. The useful part of the stem is its textile fibre, which easily separates from the ligneous portion, after a steeping of two or three weeks, and of this fibre ropes and coarse fabrics of the greatest strength are made. After bleaching of the combed fibre, carpets with white and brown stripes have been made of it.

A M. Van dor Scheldon recommended, in 1866, the following process for making a coarse cloth of good quality from the fibre of the hop. After the flowers have been gathered, the stalks are cut, made into bundles, and steeped like hemp. The maceration is the most important operation; for if it is not done with proper care, it is very difficult to separate the threads of the bark from the woody fibre. When the stalks have been well steeped, they are dried in the sun, beaten like hemp with a wooden mallet, and thus the threads are loosened easily. They are then carded, and are ready for weaving in the usual way. By this means a strong cloth is obtained. The thickest stalks also produce a thread suitable for the manufacture of rope.

The young sprouts or shoots, although slightly bitter, are sometimes cooked and eaten like asparagus; and the roots, according to Lindley, have been employed as a substitute for sarsaparilla.

A farmer in the north of France, having been driven by the scarcity of fodder to try to make use of whatever fell in his way for feeding his cattle, proved that hop leaves were a valuable element of food for cows when mixed with other substances. He found that whenever he gave them hop leaves he always obtained more milk, and his cows throve better than usual. The leaves must be used as soon as they are plucked, for the cows object to them when dried by the sun.

The hop bine has often been suggested as a paper material, but no practical action has yet been taken on any extensive scale in the matter.

In 1838, George Robert D'Harcourt included it in a patent among various other substances; and in the following year Thomas MacGauran also patented paper-making from hop bine, either by itself, or mixed with other suitable material. Again, in 1854, Thomas L. Holt and William Charlton obtained provisional protection for using the hop stem or bine with other plants, either alone or combined with rags.

In 1845, a patent was taken out for using spent hops from the breweries for paper-making.

An invention of Mr. Henry Dyer, of Camberwell, recently published, describes improvements in the manufacture of pulp for paper-making, and consists in the application and employment as materials for this purpose of spent hops or spent malt from breweries or distilleries, either together or separately, in combination or not with other materials, such as cotton, linen, hemp, woollen or silk rags, or esparto, diss, palm leaves, straw, wood pulp, jute, gunny, manilla, Indian grass, and waste paper.

The spent hops and malt, whether employed together or separately, and with or without the other substances referred to, are to be treated by the processes and machinery usually employed for boiling, pulping, and bleaching the ordinary materials used for paper-making, and when converted into pulp may be at once made into paper, or compressed and dried for sale as half-stuff.

Instead of spent hops, fresh hops may be used, in the case of an over-abundant supply, or of a crop unfit for brewing purposes on account of blight or other causes.

The proportions of the different substances would be readily understood by paper-makers, and may be varied to suit their various requirements.

This invention claims to utilize materials hitherto valueless for any purpose except as a manure.

The claim protected by the patent is, the application and employment for the manufacture of pulp for paper-making of spent or fresh hops or spent malt, either alone or together, or in combination or not with other materials ordinarily used for paper-making.

At a meeting of paper-makers in France, in 1873, Messrs. Jourdeuil, Pauzot, and Gusses submitted samples of a textile material made from the bark of the hop stalk. By removing the outer skin, and subjecting it to chemicals, a textile substance was produced possessing length, suppleness, and delicacy of texture.

This is important to the hop farmer; for if the season should not prove favourable for the production of first-class hops, the paper-making material will compensate in some degree for this deficiency. No doubt the growth of hops will be introduced in future in many districts where they are not grown at present, as the large amount of material which they will supply for paper-making will alone ensure a good return for their cultivation.

The hop is also well known as a garden plant. It blossoms from June till August, and may be propagated by seed or by dividing the roots. It likes a deep, loamy soil, and is valuable as an ornamental climber over temporary arbours, trelliswork, &c, in summer, as its leaves are very large and afford a fine shade. The "white bine" and the "grey bine" are the best sorts for this purpose; they succeed each other.

The flower, forming a spiked inflorescence, gives rise to scales, at the base of which the fruit is developed, protected against humidity by the resinous and very odoriferous powder of a golden yellow, named lupuline.

In a technical point of view, hops are the principal element in the brewing industry; but being very sensible to the action of air, they easily deteriorate, in spite of the generally practised compression; the essential oil which they contain becomes rancid and engenders a mouldiness, so that they do not keep longer than a year. To overcome this difficulty, and in order to give a more presentable aspect to his merchandise, the hop merchant has recourse to sulphuring, an operation always successful, but which at the same time produces a pernicious reaction on the essential oil, which thereby undergoes a chemical conversion. Under the action of the sulphurous acid, which passes over the hops, the essential oil is oxidized, converted into valerianic acid, and combines with the sulphur to form a solid body. In this manner the oily matter of the hops is destroyed and the mouldiness prevented; but beer manufactured with sulphured hops will never be a wholesome beverage. The aroma of the hops is replaced by that of the valerianic acid, the sulphurous acid contained in the hops is partly converted into sulphuric acid, and the sulphur of commerce being arseniferous, the arsenious acid passes with the sulphurous acid in the hops, both are communicated to the beer, and may, although taken in small doses, inconvenience the consumer.

Another disadvantage is the action of the sulphurous acid on the tannic acid in converting it into gallic acid, which prevents the clarification and the fermentation of the beers, besides giving them a rough or sour flavour. The due preservation of hops with all their active and useful properties, without being subjected to sulphurous fumigation, has been the object of long researches.

Ten years ago a soft and dry extract of hops was manufactured, containing in a small volume the bitter, tonic, and aromatic principles of the plant, of which it represented very nearly the fifth. This soft extract is a kind of brownish preserve, which, as it will not keep long, the brewer docs not care to utilize; the dry extract which is still manufactured is in a coarse powder, and keeps better; it is used to improve the bitterness of beers in course of manufacture when they are too sweet.

The question that has occupied so much time has at last been solved: the preservation of hops without sulphuring and without the extraction of their bitter and tannic principles. By chemical and mechanical means the green or freshly dried hops are separated from their essential oil, the great obstacle to their preservation, so that the strobiles remain whole, keep their original colour, the yellow dust at the base of the scales, and all their bitter and tonic principles, the aroma excepted. Hops thus treated and compressed will, it is said, keep for years.

The essential oil is preserved by itself in hermetically sealed bottles, and improves from year to year.

In the manufacture of beer, one operates with these hops as usual; and after the fermentation ten or twelve drops of essential oil are added per hectolitre (22 gallons); the extraction of the bitter principle and of the tannin, the clarification and the fermentation are effected perfectly, the beer is of superior quality, very thin, limpid, clear, and creamy, being characterized by a delicious bouquet of hops, and keeps much better as, under the influence of the essential oil, the mycodemæ, microscopic animalculæ, which, by their presence in beer, cause an acetic and putrid fermentation, perish.

Chemistry of Hops.—Messrs. Payen and Chevallier, so far

back as 1830, and even before, determined that the yellow secretion of hops, a bitter and aromatic element, was the sole source of the flavour, the strong odour, and, in fact, the active principle; and that the bracts of the cones which were not touched with the yellow substance, had no more aromatic odour or flavour than dry hay. They also ascertained that this yellow powder or secretion is found in varying proportions in different kinds of hops, and hence their real and useful value differs materially.

The following is the mode in which these able chemists made the analysis, which is more mechanical than chemical. "The strobiles, or cones, of the hops are taken when well dry, and the foreign matters which they contain are separated as much as possible; they are then placed on a fine horsehair sieve, pressed with the hand, and the sieve shaken; the pulverulent secretion passes through the meshes of the sieve, leaving the bracts on the top. These are again submitted to pressure and agitation, to separate any more of the yellow powder which may have escaped, until nothing is left but the waste bracts. Care, however, must be taken not to crush or bruise these, so that none may pass through the meshes to augment the bulk of the sifted powder. This product can then be weighed and preserved in closed vessels."

Dr. Ives found, on analysis, the lupulinic grains to contain

Tannin	4·16
Extractive	8·33
Bitter principle	9·16
Wax	10·00
Resin	30·00
Lignin	38·33
Loss	·02
	100·

The following analyses are useful for reference, as showing the percentage quality of the different hops of commerce, chiefly those of the Continent:

	Foreign Matters.	Waste Bracts.	Yellow Secretion.
Poperinghe (Belgium)	12·00	70·00	18·00
Old American	14·30	68·80	16·90
Bourges	0·50	83·50	16·00
Lake Crécy (Oise)	1·80	86·20	12·00
Bussignies	7·00	81·50	11·50
Vosges	3·00	86·00	11·00
Old English	3·00	87·00	10·00
Luneville	1·50	88·50	10·00
Liege	10·00	81·00	9·00
Alost	16·00	76·00	8·00
Spalt	3·00	88·00	8·00
Toul	1·50	91·50	8·00

Turpin recognized in the glands of the hops the presence of two vesicles in which an etherized oil existed, and Raspail, by a more careful examination, found chlorophyl, a resinous substance, an etherized oil, and some gluten in them. Payen and Chevallier analyzed hops from different sources, and they found as a minimum 8 per cent., and as a maximum 18 per cent, of hop dust. It is a well-known fact that the hops of different countries are not equally good; the difference in the quantity of the yellow powder may, among others, he one of the causes; but, as in the manipulations which the hops undergo, the yellow powder may be easily detached, it would be wrong to conclude from the experiments of Payen and Chevallier, that, in the hops as they are in the field, there exists such a difference in the quantity of powder; during the carriage a small quantity may in some way or other be lost.

Wimmer found in 100 parts of hops 20 parts of powder to 80 parts of scales. But as it was impossible to separate from the flowers all the particles of yellow dust held, he was of opinion that about half more ought to be added. He found, by analysis, the following percentages:

	Folioles of the Flower.	Yellow Dust.	Folioles and Dust together.
Volatile oil	..	0·12	0·12
Tannic acid	1·6	0·7	2·3
Bitter substance	4·7	3·0	7·7
Gummy "	5·8	1·3	7·1
Resinous "	2·0	2·9	4·9
Vegetable cells	64·0	9·0	73·0
	78·1	17·02	95·12
Watery extract	12·1	4·9	17·

Lupuline.—This name has been given by Ives to the yellow dust which covers the folioles of the female flower of hops. Later on Ives, Payen, Chevallier, and Pelletan gave the same name to the bitter substance contained in the dust.

Besides the oil which is obtained by distillation, and the tannic acid, which is also not without value as regards the preparation of beer, the resin and the bitter substance especially deserve to be distinguished. They are both obtained by treating with alcohol the yellow dust of the hops. Water is added to this tincture, and it is distilled, which causes the separation of a large quantity of resin. The tannic acid and malie acid are saturated by means of lime, and the liquor is evaporated. If the residue is treated by ether to further obtain a small remaining quantity of resin, then by alcohol, the bitter substance dissolves in the alcohol, and may be separated from it by evaporation.

Lupuline, seen under the miscroscope, resembles an acorn in its cupule; it is a gland composed of a hidden cupule, surrounded by a membraneous sac, called the *cuticule*, which contains the products of the secretion, constituting the essential oil of hops.

This essential oil is a clear green liquid, slightly bitter, very aromatic, of the mellow odour of fresh hops; its specific weight = 908 at + 16° C.; it is but slightly soluble in water, very soluble in alcohol, and boils at + 240° C. Iodine and bromine turn it brown and alcoholized sulphuric acid reddens it. The essential oil is composed of an eleoptine and a stearoptine. The eleoptine is a hydrocarbon, $C^{10}H^{8}$, isometric with spirits of turpentine, and distils at + 175° C. The stearoptine is an oxygenized hydrocarbon $C^{10}H^{12}O^{2}$, isomeric with valerol, which distils at + 210° C., and is converted by oxidation into valerianic acid.

> The chemical composition of lupuline proves the richness of its principles, for analysis has found in it the following:

1. Water.
2. Essential oil.
3. Acetate of ammonia.
4. Malate of lime.
5. Albumine.
6. Gum.
7. Malic acid.
8. Tannic acid.
9. A resin.
10. Bitter extract.
11. A fatty matter.
12. Chlorophyl.
13. Acetate of lime.
14. Nitrate and sulphate of potash.

15. Sub-carbonate of potash.
16. Carbonate and phosphate of lime.
17. Phosphate of magnesia.
18. Sulphur.
19. Oxide of iron.
20. Silica.

In therapeutics, lupuline plays an important part, but the properties of the etherized narcotic extract, and those of a crystalline acid, in very bitter silky needles, which might be called humulin, have never been experimented on, and would probably be found powerful substitutes for opium and quinine.

The *bitter substance of hops* is a yellow solid matter, not very soluble in water, easily soluble in alcohol, less soluble in ether; it is odourless and of a very bitter flavour; has a feeble tendency to combine as easily with the metallic bases as with the acids. The *resin of hops* may be obtained pure by the action of boiling water. In the pure state this resin is free from all bitter flavour, it is insoluble in water; but is, on the contrary, very soluble in alcohol and in ether. The resin of hops has been the object of research by Vlaanderen. He treated the hop dust with boiling alcohol, then filtered it, added a considerable quantity of water, and evaporated it. In the yellow, cloudy liquor a soft resin of a dark brown colour is thrown down; this is separated from the liquor, again dissolved in alcohol, filtered, once more mixed with a large quantity of water, and evaporated, for the purpose of separating as much as possible by this evaporation the oil which remains adhering to the resin. The same treatment is recommended several times, and continued until the resin has lost all trace of bitterness.

The *etherized oil of hops* is a yellow oil, obtained, it is said, in the proportion of 2 per cent, from hop dust by distillation. I have, however, never seen it obtained in such a quantity. The resin retains moreover a very large quantity of oil. This volatile oil is more or less soluble in water, it easily dissolves in alcohol and in ether. Its specific weight has been found = 0.908.

Way and Ogston on the one hand, and Hawkhurst on the other, have determined by analysis the constituent inorganic parts of hops. Watts and Nesbit have also effected the determination of them.

The following are their respective analyses:

	Way and Ogston.		Hawkhurst.	Nesbit.
Potass	12	25	19·4	25·2
Chloride of potassium	5	..	..	1·7
,, sodium	..	3	..	7·2
Lime	18	22	14·2	16·0
Magnesia	6	5	6·3	6·8
Sesqui-oxide of iron	2	2	2·7	7·5
				Phosphate of Sesqui-oxide of Iron.
Phosphoric acid	21	14	14·6	9·8
Sulphuric ,, ...	7	7	8·3	5·4
Silicic ,, ...	23	20	17·9	21·5
Carbonic ,, ...	5	2	11·0	..
Soda	..	..	0·7	..
Alumina	..	..	1·2	..
Chlorine	..	..	2·3	..
Amount of ash per cent. ..	8	6	..	..

It is chiefly to its bitter principle that the physiological action which hops exert is generally due; this action has been compared to that of opium, and a narcotic power is generally attributed to bops, but I do not find sufficient reasons for this assertion.

In 1863 Lermer suggested the presence of a peculiar alkaloid in hops. Griessmayer's recent experiments seem to prove the existence of a peculiar volatile alkaloid, which he named lupulina. The concentrated aqueous decoction of ten pounds of hops was distilled with potassa or with magnesia, the distillate neutralised with muriatic acid, evaporated to dryness, treated with cold absolute alcohol, to remove sal-ammoniac, the alcoholic liquid heated to boiling, and evolved, when much muriate of trimethylamina crystallized. The filtrate evaporated in a water-bath, and finally spontaneously, the residue redissolved in water, in a narrow cylinder, agitated with potassa and ether, and the ethereal solution evaporated spontaneously. The remaining alkaline liquid had a peculiar odour, reminding of conia, and a cooling but not bitter taste. It soon separated in small crystals, and finally solidified completely. Other experiments proved that some kinds of hops contain no trimethylamina, and finally, also, that the substances present in hops go into beer.

MEDICINAL USES OF HOPS

HOPS are used medicinally for their stomachic and tonic properties. They are also to some extent suporific, especially the odorous vapours from them; hence a pillow stuffed with hops is occasionally employed as an agreeable sedative to induce sleep, and was obtained for George III. when a lunatic. The extract has been found to allay pain; but after all, it is a better adjunct to beer than as a medicine. The infusion and tincture act as pleasant aromatic tonics, but Pereira doubts the existence of the narcotic effects which have been ascribed to hops.

He, however, states that the medicinal properties of hops are numerous. Both infusion and tincture of hops are mild and agreeable aromatic tonics. They sometimes manifest diuretic, or when the skin is kept warm, sudorific qualities. Their sedative, soporific, and anodyne properties are, however, very uncertain. Hops have been given internally to relieve restlessness consequent upon exhaustion or fatigue, to induce sleep in the wakefulness of mania and other maladies; to calm nervous irritation, and to relieve pain in gout and rheumatism. They have also been applied topically in the form of a fomentation or poultice, as a resolvent or discutient in painful swellings or tumours.

As the narcotic properties are due to the volatile oil, hops should be obtained as fresh as possible; and the medicinal tincture made from a fresh, well-matured hop is preferable to one made from old lupuline, although it would not be as uniform in strength, from the great range in quality; but as it is difficult to obtain either hops or lupuline fresh at all times, the lupuline is preferable, as it is of more uniform strength, and retains its properties longer. The hop, when old, is of very unequal strength, from the loss of lupuline sifted out in handling. For pharmaceutical use hops are pressed into quarter-pound, half-pound, and pound packages.

It is somewhat remarkable that lupuline has not found a place in the new Pharmacopoeia of this country. It may, however, be said that it is not altogether ignored, inasmuch as it is extracted for that purpose, but the amount of it in different samples varies considerably, and it is certain that this peculiar powdery matter represents the active principles of the entire strobili in a concentrated form.

In order to free lupuline from sand, which often contaminates it, Sarrazin proposes to wash it with water. The lupuline was several times suspended in 10 parts of water, and poured off rapidly. It was then collected on a filter, and dried on it, at between 77° and 86° Fahr. From 5 grams he obtained 34 grains of purified lupuline, and the washings only contained between 2 and 3 grains of extract. The medicinal effect of the lupuline was not affected by the washing. Sarrazin* also proposes a liquid extract prepared as follows:

Thirty parts lupuline are macerated in 100 parts alcohol for two days, filtered, the residue washed with a little more alcohol, and then infused in 200 parts water, strained, and evaporated on a steambath, the alcoholic extract being in the meantime evaporated at a temperature between 68° and 77° Fahr. The properly concentrated liquids are mixed and brought to the measure of 45 parts. The preparation, which is effective, requires shaking before dispensing it.*

Dr. Dyce Duckworth, in a communication to the 'Pharmaceutical Journal,' in 1868,† remarks:

"It is always desirable to possess the most powerful and concentrated preparation of the vegetable Materia Medica, and as no available active principle has as yet been separated from the hop, it should, in the meantime, be the endeavour of the pharmaceutist to obtain, and the physician to employ, the drug in its most complete and essential form. Hence I behove that at least one preparation of lupuline should be in use.

"The powder itself is inconvenient—from seven to twelve grains are requisite for a dose, and it must be given in the form of pill. In this way, too, an amount of lignin and other inert principles are ingested, which it is not desirable to employ, and which, in certain cases of gastric disease, would bo positively harmful.

"This substance appears to be most fully appreciated in the United States of America. In the authorized codex of that country, I find there are no fewer than three preparations of it: a tincture, prepared with rectified spirit; a liquid extract (corresponding in strength to those of the 'Pharmacopoeia Britannica,' viz. part for part); and an oleo-resin. The French Codex takes no notice of it. In the Edinburgh Pharmacopœia, there was a tincture made with rectified sprit; and lupuline was officinal in the Dublin Pharmacopœia.

"During a recent series of pharmaceutical experiments with the powder, I was constantly struck with the remarkable valerian-like odour evolved from the different preparations, and I was much interested to find, in the course of subseqnent reading on the subject, that M, Personne had discovered valerianic acid in lupuline.*

"In none of the British Pharmacopœia preparations of hops, except the extract, can it be said that the real strength of the drug is removed. The tincture made with proof spirit, which does not thoroughly exhaust the active parts of the scales of lupuline, and the watery infusion can but inadequately represent the virtues of this medicine.

"The extract of hops, as prepared partly with spirit like the extract of jalap, has the advantage of containing some resin and volatile oil. It is the presence in so considerable an amount of resin, gum, and wax, in lupuline, that renders it important to select a proper solvent, and therefore proof spirit and water respectively are incapable of acting thoroughly upon it. We may, indeed, practically regard lupuline as a gum-resin, and to treat it pharmaceutically with success, we must apply the same solvents as we do in the case of drugs of that class. I have devised a preparation, which I think will prove most useful whenever it is desired to use the hop. It is an ammoniated tincture, and should be made in the same way as the other ammoniated tinctures of the Pharmacopœia.

"Like valerian, which also contains an oil and a resin, lupuline is best exhausted by the aromatic spirit of ammonia, and the reason for this appears to be that this preparation contains the combination of alkali and rectified spirit necessary to the solution of the various elements in these drugs. Certainly no agent that I have tried extracts the virtues of lupuline so well as sal-volatile. The result is a strong, richly-coloured tincture. Neither rectified spirit, ether, nor of course proof spirit, produces so strong a preparation. I recommend the following formula:

"Lupuline, 2 oz.; spirit ammon. arom., a pint. Macerate for seven days, agitating occasionally; then filter and add sufficient of the menstruum to make up to a pint. The dose of this is from m. 20 to fl. ℥j.

"I have no hesitation in directing attention to this preparation of the hop as the best we at present possess. According to Christison, the dose of tinetura lupuli should be fl. ℥j to fl. ℥ iss, to produce any hypnotic effect; the ordinary dose consists of as many drachms. Dr. Ives, of New York, states that the tincture of lupuline is an effectual hypnotic in restlessness, the result of nervous irritability, and in delirium tremens.* Some advantage, too, is derived from the presence of ammonia in considerable quantity, and this whether the preparation be exhibited as a hypnotic, or as a tonic combination of bitter and ammonia."

Mr. C. Lewis Diehl thus prepares the elixirs prescribed by the physicians of Louisville:

Elixir of Hops.– Add 2 1/2 fluid ounces of fluid extract of hops—made according to the formula for fluid extract of gentian of United States –to 13 1/2 fluid ounces of simple elixir; mis and filter.

Elixir of Lupuline.—Triturate 2 ounces of fluid extract of lupuline with two ounces of carbonate of magnesia, add 14 fluid ounces of simple elixir, transfer to a bottle, agitate occasionally for several hours, and filter.

Extract of Hops.—In 1872, Professor C. A. Seeley, of New

York, patented in the United States and England an improved process for extracting the useful substances of hops, and for manufacturing a pure and concentrated extract of hops. The invention is based on the discovery that the ordinary petroleum oils are rapid and complete solvents of the essential oils and of the bitter matter of hops. At the same time they have no solvent action on the other constituents of the plant, which in practical operations are either useless or hurtful. The improved process consists in steeping the hops in petroleum oil, and then by heat, stirring, digestion, and percolation, promoting the solvent action of the oil. When the extractable matter of the hops has been thus dissolved, the solution of hop extract in oil is separated by filtration from the refuse matter, and the solvent is volatilized or distilled off by heat; the extract thus being obtained free from the solvent and other foreign matter.

The kinds of petroleum oil proper for this purpose are naphtha and gasoline, which are the lighter and more volatile parts of crude Pennsylvania petroleum. Although any petroleum oil which has a boiling point below 212° Fahr, may be used, a gasoline which boils at about 100° Fahr, is preferable, because at that temperature the essential oil of hops will not escape from the extract solution when distilling the solvent.

The apparatus employed in manufacturing the solution

and distilling the solvent is such as is suitable and well known for use where bisulphide of carbon, ether, hydrocarbons, or alcohol is used for analogous purposes. The extract of hops prepared as I have described 13 of a pasty consistency, more or less thin in proportion to the essential oil contained in it.

It is soluble in water, but slowly and only in small quantity. In order to increase its solubility in water, and to give it a more convenient consistency for measuring and transferring, sufficient alcohol is added to give it the consistency of thin syrup. This is probably the best form for a commercial extract of hops. This hop extract differs in some important respects from the extracts of hops hitherto known, and is therefore a new commercial product. It contains all the matter of the hop plant which it is desirable to use in the preparation of beer; while the saline and albumenoid substances found in alcoholic and watery extracts are wholly absent from it. The extract in its simple form is solid when cold, pasty when warm, and quite fluid at the boiling point of water."

Mr. Emmet Kannal, in the 'American Journal of Pharmacy,' gives the following recipe to prepare glycerole of lupuline:

"Take of Inpuline 1 troy ounce, alcohol 6 fluid ounces, glycerine 9 fluid ouneos, Curaçoa cordial 1 fluid ounce.

"Mix the alcohol with 2 fluid ounces of glycorine, moisten

the lupuline with the mixturc, pack it into a cylindrical percolator, and continue to add this mixture until 8 fluid ounces of the percolate has passed; to this add the remainder of glycerine, previously mixed with the Curaçoa, and thoroughly mix the whole together. This will afford by careful manipulation a very fine preparation miscible with any of the ordinary syrups or tinctures, and possessing all the medicinal properties of lupuline.

"Dose for an adult one teaspoonful, representing 7 1/2 graius of lupuline."

According to Wagner ('Chemical Technology'), the essential oil, the flavouring principle of the hops, is met with in air-dried hops, to the amount of 0·8 per cent.; it is yellow-coloured, with an acrid taste, without narcotic effect, of a specific gravity = 0·908, turning litmus paper red. It requires more than 600 times its weight of water to effect a solution. It is free from sulphur, and belongs to the group of essential oils characterized by the formula C_5H_8, and can become oxidized under contact with the air into valerianic acid ($C_5H_{10}O_2$), this oxidation being the cause of the peculiar cheesy odour of old hops; it is a mixture of a hydrocarbon C_5H_8 isomeric with the oils of turpentine and rosemary, with an oil containing oxygen $C_{10}H_{18}O$, having the property of oxidation alluded to.

Tannic acid is found in the several kinds of hops, in quantities varying from two to three per cent., and is an important constituent, as it precipitates the albuminous matter of the barley, and serves to clear the liquor. It gives with the persalts of iron a green precipitate; treated with acids and synaptase, does not separate into gallic acid and sugar; and by dry distillation, does not give any pyrogallic acid. The hop resin is the important constituent of the hops, and contains the bitter principle or lupuline. It is difficultly soluble in water, especially in pure water, and when the lupuline or essential oil is absent. But water containing tannic acid, gums, and sugar dissolves a considerable quantity of the resin, especially when the essential oil is present. It is intensely bitter in taste, and becomes foliated when exposed to the atmosphere.

Hop resin and the essential oil are not identical; the former is soluble in ether, the latter is not. In the course of long exposure it becomes insoluble. The gum and extractive colouring matter are of little use. The mineral constituents of hops dried at 100° are: ash, 9 to 10 per cent.; 15 per cent, of phosphoric acid; 17 per cent, of potash, &c.

Hops have recently been found to be a photo preservative. Numerous experiments having been made in the emulsion process, the desideratum has been found in ordinary hops — preferably the variety known as Bavarian, which seems stronger in certain qualities than the English hop. According to the 'British Journal of Photography':

"Two ounces of hops are infused for one hour in 20 ounces of water at a temperature of 170° Fahr., and the whole then turned into a cloth, and the liquid pressed out. When cold, 20 grains of pyrogallic acid and the albumen of two eggs are added, and the mixture is well shaken for ten minutes. It is then filtered into a dish and used in the ordinary way; or, if only a few plates are to be prepared, a smaller quantity may be made, and poured off and on several times. Plates preserved with this solution dry perfectly hard, have a fine gloss, and yield negatives of very high quality. The colour is a rich greenish-brown, and so non-actinic that over-development must be carefully guarded against. Although the solution can be easily made, it is desirable that, if possible, it should be made to keep, and therefore we have added carbolic acid and salicylic acid to separate quantities, and shall note the result on a future occasion.

"Meantime we consider the hop preservative, as abovo indicated, a decided improvement on the beer and albumen. It possesses all its good, without any of its bad, qualities; the principal of which are the stickiness already referred to, the varying qualities of beer in different localities, and, especially, the irregular proportions of chlorides which, more or less, are always present, and to get rid of which many workers are in the habit of adding silver nitrate, which always introduces an additional element of uncertainty."

* 'Arch. Phar.,' Oct. 1874, p. 333.

* 'Arch. Phar.,' Oct, 1875, p. 331.

† Vol. x., Second Series, p. 246.

* 'Comptes Rendus,' 1854.

* *Vide* American Codex, also Nevin's 'Translation of Lond. Pharm., 1851.

CPSIA information can be obtained at www.ICGtesting.com
Printed in the USA
LVOW10s0849080216

474163LV00001B/39/P